A Rotating Equipment Engineer is Never Finished

A Rotating Equipment Engineer is Never Finished

John Milkereit

INK
BRUSH
PRESS

ISBN: 978-0-9909452-0-8
Library of Congress Control Number: 2015935133

Manufactured in the United States

Ink Brush Press
Dallas, Texas

For Mom and Dad

Poetry from Ink Brush Press

Alan Birkelbach and Karla Morton, *No End of Vision: Texas as
   Seen by Two Laureates*
David Bowles, *Shattering and Bricolage*
Jerry Bradley, *The Importance of Elsewhere*
Millard Dunn, *Places We Could Never Find Alone*
Dede Fox, *Postcards Home*
Chris Ellery, *The Big Mosque of Mercy*
Alan Gann, *Adventures of the Clumsy Juggler*
Charles Inge, *Brazos View*
Robin McCorquodale, *Falling Into Harmony*
Jim McGarrah, *Breakfast at Denny's*
J. Pittman McGehee, *Growing Down*
Steven Schroeder, *a dim sum of the day before*
Steven Schroeder and Sou Vai Keng, *a guest giving way like ice melting*
Jan Seale, *Nape*
Jan Seale, *The Wonder Is*
W.K. Stratton. *Dreaming Sam Peckinpah*
Chuck Taylor, *At the Heart*
Jesse Waters, *Human Resources*
Scott Yarbrough, *A Sort of Adam Infant Dropped: True Myths*

For information on these and other Ink Brush Press books go to
www.inkbrushpress.com

Acknowledgments

I am grateful to the editors of the following journals, chapbooks, and anthologies where these poems first appeared.

Poetry at Round Top
Swirl
di-verse-city (2013 anthology)
Houston Poetry Festival (anthologies of 2010-2013)
The Texas Poetry Calendar 2011
Inprint Annual Report, 2007-2008
The Weight of Addition, an Anthology of Texas Poetry
San Pedro River Review
Harbinger Asylum
Home & Away
Paying Admissions

For critique and support, I am grateful to know members of three poetry groups. The first is Net Poet Society, which has met every other Monday for the past six years and during the first few hyper years also via email. The second group is, for lack of a better name, The Tuesday Night Group. The third group, is the Inner Loopers, which meets inside IH-610. The first two groups formed from workshops originally organized by Inprint, a non-profit organization in Houston that supports the literary arts. My gratitude also extends to the magical city of San Miguel, Mexico and all the participants of the San Miguel Poetry Week.

I thank Sarah Cortez for her crucial organization of this book in its initial form, and also poets Dave Parsons, Randall Watson, Lola Haskins, and Sasha West for their poetic insights. Bruce Bode, a Unitarian Universalist minister, first opened my eyes to the gift of poetry after I attended a seminar.

My friends and family have offered plenty of encouragement that I will forever remember and appreciate.

CONTENTS

How Things Work

Digging Quiet Holes

Little Drownings

Forcing My Soul into Knives

Notes

How Things Work

Rotating Equipment Engineer

He enters his office
from a hallway, dimly lit
with a sack lunch
ready to say no.

His *I-don't-build-anything*
kind of job description.
What he actually does is mystery.
One morning, his glasses reflect from a computer screen
a motor data sheet or news that a volcano erupted in Indonesia–

you would never know for sure. Poems ought to turn
as much as the pumps he specifies. Words and shafts
are traitors and dirty when the start button is pressed.
Parts spin out of control, taking limbs off their operators.
There were the days when he made more money

than a doctor, when building factories was a revolution.
His metal is so much like the sentence that takes so long
to get poured, and welded, and bolted into its shape.
Why not turn the result
over to the rulers of the world?

He always waits with a red pen mounted on his keyboard
ready to reject a test.
In a pair of steel-toed boots, he can fly to a factory
to witness what is ready to ship.
No matter what he calculates,
whatever tools are hidden in his pocket,
he is never finished.

Ode to Mathematics

Without disguise
unresolved on white pages
by the radiator overlooking the alley
or on the chalkboard by the door
when the desk remembered
the stillness of the forest,
you appeared.
When older textbooks reached
further past the same quiet,
they winced, cut like this,
containing ink for numbers, symbols,
some sort of solution.

You're real,
not imaginary, from nothing
to infinity
at the library under the shaded area
which could have disturbed you.
But what about the time when calculators
no longer worked because you embraced
x's, and y's
eliminating intuition,
acting as a chameleon, granular skin,
derivatives of color,
as each new problem becomes more absurd?
They were not your stories.
Were trains A or B ever going to Poughkeepsie?
Was anything going anywhere?

Your flash cards are gone.
Endless programming loops truncate

at eyes of windows.
Adjusting those rooms
we touch or measure,
you enter and leave as you wish,
unabashed.

Inertia

spun me around in Mr. Olasov's physics class where I always looked at the clock. I never wanted to attend whether I became stupid or suddenly smart in a private little school across from a cemetery in Charleston you thought Marilyn Monroe would slide by in a carriage from a Civil War scene. Osmosis said, filtered down, that I was miserable, drawing flowers on gravestones, spotting the occasional mockingbird chirping her voice. My head became a little experiment, rolling, like fluid in a flask. Willy Nelson blared "On the Road Again" from a redneck pick-up truck. Henry the Eighth would have been ashamed or sick. I connected the dots, the lines made the Pythagorean theorem work. I heated my body against a blonde cheerleader; cupped her in the tiny school parking lot frequented by bad boys smoking pot. Some were listening to Michael Jackson when it was cool on thin, fancy car radios their fathers bought them if they lived south of Tradd Street. I was busy becoming a sort of student learning the 1st law of thermodynamics and the 2nd and 3rd and whatever else Mr. Olasov emitted, now long forgotten. We never heard music, no Yo-Yo Ma–he came to the festival for chamber music that floated like silk into balconies and landed with the force of gravity in ear-drummed peninsulas of sound strung from each other, gravitated into the light of space that replaced Horowitz and cancelled any affection for Elvis, his fried peanut butter and banana sandwiches, and his streaked pool table last seen sprinting across memory. Other light rocketed, sketched upwards and never returned, never came back.

Aurora

I captured your pictures,
       goddess of dawn,
electronic wisps
    descending from space
colliding with molecules from the upper arc
in the atmosphere of my local post office
     on a plate of stamps
that shows cuts of your *australis*,
       your *borealis*.

You say the curtains of your phenomena
aren't for my eyes, no magnetic attraction
where I reside,
no green or red ray of emission
is possible unless your intensity leaks
to my lower state,
and if so, will I
be present to receive your drink
of polar noiselessness
that spills and would spill
but never completely spills?

I cannot lick the curve of your back
you're unglueable
your return hinges
on fields unpredictable, but I will
await your runs across the sky,
fixed, or unfixed
over the mountains knifed
north a little longer and air mail
this envelope with an inked,
colorless storm
    metered.

Middle-Aged Man Driving Through Indiana

I'm paying tolls
past the old Falstaff brewery
and the Gary flares in a rental car
recalling pine-sapped Elkhart kisses.

If I were younger, I would have written
a terrible verse of hoppy-stench aroma
drunk at the ballpark and tossed a bitter line
over why we never rounded the bases.

So much better now, decades later–
forgetting the wish you were here
in Pink Floyd's "Wish You Were Here"
and describing colder, lime-wedged beer

and absorbing dark-roomed chemicals
my great-grandfather used for printing farm
photographs. Farms spill memoirish smells
past Purdue, even corn syrup burning

near the ethanol plant,
and the granite hat that I
now place over another relative
after turning right at the IGA.

I wave goodbye to Big Boy
and the strawberries never picked
in Michigan City on the way back
to Chicago bottled light with change.

Introduction to Dating Women for More Than Six Months

I remember the mind-numbing
religious dogma, but mostly scenes
in my car–always a soap opera. I
tired from the yellow throat of her psycho
dog, Andy, who barked at chairs,
leather swanky couches, and snapped
at plaid shirts. I saw hallways
ribbed in red, my head floundering,
vines falling fast, more like having
a sleep disorder at an aquarium.

I tried delivering lilies in a cowboy hat
from the squatty florist near
the freeway, transporting pink trumpets
and surviving an hourglass full
before weekends were covered over
and enough energy was expended to drain
a condominium. She introduced me to sinking–
into the charged cave of an eel?

A year later, after murky indecision,
I raced a Dale-Earnhardt way out
and married a house. I see her dating
a tow truck driver who decks the Court
at Lily Way. She never spoke diehard
negative, or how elements draw together.
I try to remember how fragile cells exist.

Blues Song

B.B. King sung on this riddled December night
that you are a million miles away after leaving
town with another man, baby. You fed
me breakfast every day,

but after a guitar riff
and another taste of Australian Shiraz,
I realize 197 miles separate us
after you left with a man you already knew.

You wouldn't have wanted me
to call you *baby*, *sugar*, or *my little girl*.

You fed me the night constellation
on a beach blanket, the wind through hair
as we bicycled along a bayou,
and that stare across a crowded hallway.
Eggs, never scrambled with you,
we didn't lived together
or smoke cigarettes.

In a holiday card,
she announces a baby boy.
I don't know what to do now
except finish the wine
and tell the person upstairs
to stop playing the violin.

On a Sunny Afternoon I Think of Grant Wood

I'm whispering about Grant Wood–
threadbare, stooped over the farmhouse sketch
for his *American Gothic*,
the double portrait of his sister Nan and his dentist,
under a sky denim faded,
sunlight coming down like a calico curtain,
a potted geranium and a sasevieria
playing make-believe on the porch.

Wood hasn't painted
a *Portrait of Nan*,
a sort of apology to show his sister's face
wouldn't turn milk sour. He hasn't
traded his overalls for an artist's smock yet
either. He's Grant Wood and all his really
good ideas come while milking cows.
And already he's painted his mother
holding a potted snake plant, and the backside
of a spotted naked man. He's thirty-eight.
And now pitchforks.

I'm thinking of Grant Wood because my dentist
is about to take X-rays. My teeth
are chickens, my bone a little sheaf of grain,
my mouth a split-open plum
waiting for an implant, titanium grade No. 4.
I'm excited but more like the chick in Nan's portrait–
hungry, fussy, closeted–as if I'm lost. Like toast without
butter. Or potatoes, no gravy.

When the dental assistant in her purple scrubs
begins, "Do you take any diet pills?"
I could strangle her. "What about heart medication?"
As if my arteries are propped open. As if my arteries
aren't model portraits. As if they were like dark vessels.
Like the cherry tree hatcheted in *Parson Weem's Fable*,
like the mangled road in the *Midnight Ride of Paul Revere*,
like the dirt in *Spring Plowing*. All of these dark Wood paintings.
Like the farmer's jacket. Like space in a jawbone.

Self-Portrait After Seeing Gunilla Klingberg's *Wheel of Everyday Life*

Is there a hole in my brain because of the ozone layer,
or is it because I've never watched the *Today Show*?

I've been eating my life away one slice
of Star Pizza's Joes at a time–
spinach, garlic, and whole wheat crust.

I want Comet on my soul
so I can get to Wal-Mart without being
trampled on Black Friday.

I buy beer at Target because they verify I'm at least 21.
My heart chakra is made from ten-piece, chicken-tender
meals from Dairy Queen with honey mustard and not enough
BBQ sauce.

My 1 lb. bag of Imperial Sugar will outlive a gorilla.
I feed my car a tank of gasoline at Texaco
without going to Shipley's Donuts. When my arm
retracts into the shell of my body, I revert to my
faith-based initiative of looking from any window.

Oh My God. I'm so happy about Target that I return to buy
low-fat CHEEZ-ITs!

K-Mart is like a fiesta. It is a horrible country
road, like us, filled with chug holes. It is not sweet mandolin music.

I keep going and going in circles until I find Energizer
stickers at this cosmos' edge. A white bunny
marches, clanging his cymbals.

Once, I dreamt that I was in the underworld like Orpheus,
and when I turned to see Eurydice, she became
a 12-pack of Charmin.

Mozart, Tanned Legs, Jasmine

When I visited the psychotherapist in the silk dress,
she became a mustached barber in a silver smock
laughing near a plain M&M candy machine,
and when I visited the 18th green of the golf course
with the waves coasting in behind the ledges,
the scene became a horse saddled
galloping in place on a merry-go-round.
My mind was playing tricks,
firing incorrect pictures
turning spinach lasagna into sparrows
and French literature from 1895 to 1914 into expresso,
for when I visited a used Cadillac lot,
it became a field of Stonehenge replicated
by two visionary cowboys,
and when I visited a woodpecker in a chinaberry tree,
Gandhi began marching for salt,
and when I visited a place, finally, where everyone lived
in harmony, that became only a truck stop with an island
of broken gas pumps.
Once, I trusted the mind despite its trappings
with reliable synapses, and I was blessed to live in a god-forsaken
suburb of the mind,
I wanted Mozart, tanned legs, and jasmine to charge and infuse it,
and I roamed through swamps yearning for joy
and ran through a park yearning for euphoria.
Today when I sit still, I see bursts of lightning
ebbing and pulsing
and I see a leaf falling back and forth from an unknown tree
and I see snow flakes falling like laced gowns on the hill
I once sled,
I want to make everything better now.

I want to make the psychotherapist in the white dress
stop her talking and stop her listening,
and I want to make the horse come alive,
and I want to make kisses with a sparrow.
I want to make my shadow, my beat-up shadow
wear a ripped white linen shirt, and drive to the airport
laughing and laughing
with her clipped hair.

Career Checklist

A. You grow up and become something.

B. Your hands are clean.

C. Work is not a game of Monopoly.

D. Starve if you're not in a bubble.

E. You tested as the BORE type.

F. A vise grip locks and feels okay.

G. Your nose is safe.

H. Office curtains are closed and you remain on the bottom.

I. Changing careers means schooling was charades.

J. The first friend colors you *bland*.

K. Fluctuations in the economy mean you're a sardine.

L. A resume is the history of flicking marbles.

M. Driving an empty vehicle is exciting.

N. The best source of job leads is your want.

O. Your second friend is Oprah.

P. You love creamy peanut butter and banana sandwiches.

Q. 70% of the tropical soils and oceanic release of nitrous oxide flares into euphoria unless you're pregnant.

R. Hand sanitizers outside bathrooms should have been defibrillators.

S. Metal shards from your engine explode and you're blind.

T. You cannot push a rope.

U. Buy a mobile home in Elkhart, Indiana.

V. Jesus is in the copy machine.

X. The alarm is never set.

Y. Having sex with the cleaning woman is acceptable on Thursdays.

Z. Your response to this survey is important.

The Lettuce

was in a clear bag. Sunrays hit off one side.
I remember it stuck to my hand, given by her.
I walked to school. Now I don't have the bag
or the lettuce. Did I drop it? Why would it slip?
Was it wind? I knew how to tie my shoes
before most. Knew how to spell my last
name. I knew my address, 39 Waldorf Drive.
If I know all this, then why don't I know
what happened to the bag? It was my day
to bring lettuce. The rabbit, what happens now?
Was the lettuce gobbled up by the street? Was it
run over, flattened by trucks? Do I get punished?
Do we watch the rabbit die in quiet time?
If the rabbit dies, will we get another one?
Will I have to get more lettuce? When she
finds out the lettuce got lost, will I be given
another chance–because I want to feel
counted on. That's what he said, *to be counted on*.
That means I killed something.
Something the boys and girls
who didn't know how to tie shoes, loved.
I helped them tie their shoes. They'll
find out I wasn't so smart.

Magazine

Season's greetings to the blonde on the front cover posing in her winter sonata.

On the next pages, Ali and Bono would make great parents carrying their
Louis Vuitton bags through an African field.

One of them must have landed the prop plane at dusk. The moon is invisible.

What follows are men and a young girl in front of the Mercedes. Jesus has made them
special in Tommy Hilfiger jackets.

The hush puppy and a football helmet, even when they're not
together in the yellowish grass, send their warmest wishes.

Resorts with their sky parks shower in their big boutiqueness.

There are 26 pockets and hidden conduits in a travel jacket! This
is what the Six Million Dollar Man wears.

The blessed marriage of the Aztec crepes and a Prehispanic Risotto
causes the gastronomies.

The sun is now setting.

The sun's color is probably orange but not as orange or round as the football helmet.

Mirrors or windows don't reflect upon the Trafalgar Cortina leather belts.

An eclectic group of intellectuals living on a hilltop in Rome?

The possibilities are unlimited: a life together sipping tea, studying worms, and
composting on stipends.

Bon appétit eating a tamarind duck taco from the Flying Pig food truck.

Lenny Kravitz's interior design always comes from the heart. Dreams and hopes around the Bahamas are turquoise. A leitmotif of waves pitter-patters wonder.

And the moon that won't go away is beginning to look like country.

The stars aren't indigo because the city is eating lobster with Sichuan chili sauce and black bean dust.

United works right at flying nouveau hard on the back cover with all their love and prayers.

Re: Our Conversation

Our research tells us that you or someone you know
has a select need for a borescope. You likely already know
about aircraft engines and gas turbines. You're aware of
critical interior surfaces and through-holes
because you or someone you know has access
to cavities which are all around us. Have you ever tried
to inspect compressed air inlets without disassembly?
We thought not. Imagine eliminating burrs as long as you're
willing to try our flexible or more advanced video
borescope. We would like to make a presentation in front
of you and all the people you know because then you would
see. We would offer a free box lunch that contains oleic
acid. You would see the optical beauty of our model XJ-101
after research was pressed forward into this decade by people
who have given their lives. Their interior light was held up from
their edges and poured into an innovation we cannot
reveal. This model would be considered an *endoscope*,
but it's not for the human body. It's for machinery that you
or someone you already know who is committed to the discovery
of defects in dark spaces. We don't pretend to know all of your
intended uses–maybe you would purchase as a gift, or give
the gift of seeing fuel injectors. Think of the children who will go
to Mars. Before our technology, you could never imagine the clarity
and access granted into the interior bore of a firearm. We suspect
that you or someone close to you has above average intelligence
and would leverage the increased pixels due to fibers now in the
15,000 to 22,000 range. We think you can use this device to fiberscope
your vacuum cleaner. With enough lubricant along the insertion tube,
you could capture video of remote marine life that would make
Jacques Cousteau obsolete. We are better suited for tasks deep
within what we already know. You cannot begin to understand
until you call.

The Not So Great Day at Google

Okay, so I biked to this interview with a sock tie.
It was not a nice afternoon. Sort of rainy.
I don't think I exactly aced anything but I have a powerful
sense of being ground into little ice cubes. I'm
drinking a shot of Jameson just so I can sleep. They could
call back. I didn't feel especially clever after so many
questions–all these survivor questions still flying around
my brain like mosquitoes–a manic interviewer tapping
away on his laptop, taking notes. He asks about a man who
pushed his car to a hotel and lost his fortune, and I'm
supposed to say what happened. I imagine an Impala
stuffed with garbage bags full of cash and then standing,
all sweaty, in front of a Darth-Vader-looking building.
I realize now he wanted a mental leap then with my jeans,
my knotted-up tie, but not a jump from the blender into a fire.
Then he says I'm shrunk nickel-size and thrown into a
blender so my density is the same as usual. What do I do
after the blades start whirling in sixty seconds? Looking
witty and working my I'm-so-energetic look, I climb atop
the blades, my center of gravity held tight on the axis.
I spin myself so thin and pointless, I design an evacuation
plan for San Francisco–just haul ass in cars for
Chrissake–and think of a programming language
to describe a chicken. If I met myself today, I would tear
my nice shirt into strips and with my belt, make a rope like
a gaucho throws and scale out of the jar. I wish people
would stop saying *it was nice meeting you.*

Shithead

There are men in black suits that want to hold
your soul like a hard-boiled egg and if all
you had to say is *Gosh, those troublemakers*
or *Those hellraisers*, then I'll forget we ever met,

and I don't care if you scratch off lottery tickets
at the Citgo, or how many fortune cookies
you ripped open to write a poem, or what you
think about oral sex with dentures.

Don't cover me with your psychotherapeutic
babble about self-esteem or your Vicodin
as if I was going to sit and wag my tail.

I'm grateful to have forgotten every time
I've used *shithead* in a heated sentence,
or any swear word, or actually anything I've
said until around nine o'clock this morning.

I've expanded my vocabulary into a crude
beauty that's coiled, ready to snap, not
shrinking, and never afraid to speak up.

Screw

Some people would say
that using the word *screw*
in a poem is more appropriate
as a noun rather than a verb

just as a bolt with a turning
Phillip's head shows
helpfulness, or progress,
but the past tense verb

takes on its artless form.
It's obscene, a crudeness
that drops like a meteorite
crashing through Earth's layers

to crater a front porch,
centered on the rocking chair,
behind the metal wind chimes,
the often-stolen pots of hanging ferns.

If you were sitting drinking lemonade
when the rock hit your coaster
like a fireball, wouldn't that be
the first word you'd utter?

Wouldn't you cuss, or at least regret
again the wolves howling at your gray matter
that you could've, would've, should've
had a gin and tonic?

If you remained silent, then you've
screwed up my poem and your 401K.
Humans carry toolboxes and if you can't
find exactly the right word to spend on

the exact moment, the nature
of two bodies coming close,
wood or flesh, when friction
begins, hardware oval

and flat, then I'm too poor
to help you. I see a word
that's reliable to pin
what I love, force making skin,

and when I *screw* there's heat,
a collision, a shower, a drill
raining upon a meteorite,
fastening dust to the sea.

Digging Quiet Holes

Love Poem

Poetry is...great for getting phone numbers.
                                        –Wynton Marsalis

I would rather just make you a phone. Endless minutes
with a ring tone of that rescued kitten. Why don't
I make you a phone that you can't put down, which
also jams other callers. Why don't I wear a hard hat?
My calloused hands want to help–handyman hands,
which make concertos of insurance and retirement
funds. Why don't I wake up with a dirty hard hat
that gets an orchestra on coffee? Why don't I wash
your dishes? Get Palmolive cleaning your losses, dry
tears, and laundry. Why don't I make you silence?
Knowing when to say nothing, getting into jeans
and work boots to dig quiet holes. Why don't I fill up
your noisy chambers with jars of pennies, saved up
so your heart won't wash that away, your mind
would dial me like a phone. Go ahead and ask if I
cook. I would make you tuna salad, chicken salad,
or even your favorite–egg salad. So now, look what
I'm getting you. How can you hate me?

In My Backyard

I'll build a beach with no bullying
or yodeling, and we'll surf until
a volcano blows out lawn gnomes.

I'll build a rollercoaster blowtorched
and riveted with snakes and flying mud
done with a crayoned permit.

I'll build a bust of you for that Mount Rushmore
birthday trip–that's better than a caped
gorilla bursting from a cake.

I'll build a giant remote-controlled car
from an SUV and win the swamp boil
race by avoiding the deflated tires, the wreckage.

I'll build a magnet to cover
what's wrong with tin foil
and reverse its rotation away westerly.

I'll build a home for our platypus
that protects us from Funderschmitzel's
drill-o-laters and those rodent-powered guns.

I'll build a rocketship that geysers us
to the raindow-flaked heavens. We'll never
shower a monkey or unwrap another mummy.

I'll build a laser to lay our smack-downed
faces on a comet, so when it comes around
again, we can show our grandchildren.

Sestina

What we need is thirty-nine lines, child,
and after two more, three dozen to burn
the kindling of shock and delight untied
then thirty-five left for comedians purpled
in their suits as if they're on the air,
even if their lines grow stale given dim light.

How easy it must have been for a troubadour, light
on his feet, to spew verse all over France like a child.
Then, twelfth century, compose ways to burn
song into the heads of dukes and counts untied
from wit and style until he's purple
in the face of stanzas too long on airs.

Dante took the cross to Italy's air,
so did Petrarch to continue this light
and now we're stuck in this muck of purple
obsessiveness, where lines end like a child's
fingers that seize the strings of their shoes untied.
To insist on repetition really makes love burn?

Those medieval tights should have been burned
for starters, pens should have been filled with air
not ink, more medieval days could have untied
more clothes, and hair, more affairs without candle light,
which leads to swordful playing by children
ready to become knights until their veins run purple,

or when the remains are enough for a sonnet, purpled
and unhatched like a baby who burns
for turns, where all is resolved, where as a child

squeals, and words that rhyme on the end, aired
when everyone is eating spaghetti in broad daylight
at their tables with their necklaces untied.

We're almost at the last station, so untie
us from yesteryear's events. The future is soaped lavender, even purple
as we work these iambic beats under lamplights
and play until the tambourine quits. Incense burns
as we begin to work our wants out in the air.
All we need is to visit our beds early like a child,
and include a lullaby to help burn the oil. We untie our
romance as a child does with purple ribbon. Let's launch
our kite at morning's first light into love's scattershot air.

Because You Requested Poetry About Jimi Hendrix and Eggplant

A dream must exist,
one about walking under
the flesh of a purple sea
soft and bitter.

The trip is rich and salted.
The sky acts funny as clouds
resemble five-lobed corolla
and shadows of birds oil across

whatever spell is mashed into this
brain dish. Backstage a riff plays,
the air cries out the yellow flower's
amplified release which begins the

stew of awakening in you
drifting onto an island
pollen blotted and curried
for lavender.

Making Love to Natalie Merchant

If I make love to other singers, Natalie Merchant,
the furniture isn't as elegant
and I only hear voices of idle chanting or Robert Plant.
But if we made love, the windows would rattle
and the seats would thrust back gently.
You deserve 10,000 sonnets rather than verse

orgasmically activated in rhyme of your name variant.
I know the pedals would dance on the gigantic
road where we're headed, streetlights slant
across our bodies on cruise control while clothes merrily
sing in contralto voices and fall nonchalantly
on floorboards plush carpeted as their servant.

I once read you barefooted down Sunset Blvd. perched
with only a paper bag and no ID. Is that
true? The windshield is jealous of the mirror anticipating
your face. Here, there is no LA police errant
in thinking you escaped a nuthouse. Here, the metal
hood is a carnival for the moon. Here, my elephant

ears step with admiration in the attic
between your tenor and mezzo-soprano vocals.
But honestly, this trip in my airship bluntly
means I'm dreaming. I don't want to paddle
in your kind and generous pool with antlers
thrust into you. I'm not stalking you with a Mercedes-

Benz and a pulsating label contract around Manhattan.
I haven't penned songs or sloughed pants
for you to endorse. You're married, I forgot his name,

but I bet he's no gnat buying you an antebellum
mansion where temperatures lurch the mercury.
My antenna says you are so far from the Atlantic.

I'm a legitimate adult driving to a tattoo expo but can't
decide what to buy during three ink-filled days at
the Holiday Inn. At this skin circus in Seattle
I could possess hearts & ribbons, or treble clef tats
or other streaming bubblology. Would you prefer italics?
I'll browse stencils rather defiant
in your absence. See, the tires have no simile.
The doors no longer desire change.
The dashboard darkens, and then goes nameless.

Violet

after seeing Ido Haar's *9 Star Hotel*

This is the color of our lives all backwards.
We have sex drives at 12, marry,
have children, drop out of school
after sixth grade to work in Jerusalem.

This is the color of work without a permit
we'd never get for their settlements.

God save us.

This is the color of toys thrown away
and the color of pastels tossed
and unwanted computer parts
I send back to my family in Fata.
I think of a surfboard, discarded.

We're like scavengers on some beach
in LA, no?

We're the ones who harvest olives
after the locust.

This is the color of heat under the tomatoes
with scraped bread and the sound of the late
evening flute and my sprained ankle.

I hadn't fled fast enough when they chased us.
This is the color of sirens, the color of flames
waving down our sheds.

This is the color of words
when I curse on their fathers.

When Peregrine Falcons Speed-Dated in Terminal E

You stooped above other concourses
captured pigeons in mid-air
scanned magazines
and hawked monitors
for another flight.

But today, your barred white underside
graced the chairs after Security.
When my plane was cancelled
I asked for yours.
   We taxied flights near canyon walls
in Canada or Alaska
and the best summer haunts in Colorado—
tucked trips that propelled precious duration.

We flew past the shoeshine
and over pay phone booths.
You ate my taloned grackle upside down.
We banked around,
   puddle jumped,
   darted
into marshes of desire.

But the next morning you migrated to *Mexico*?
I thought we struck an instant click,
that you were finished ducking around.
I spotted this carpet,
 steel
 and glass
as our future nest
    near abandoned gate 38.

I figured when TWA left,

                      we would spiral

home to the hope ledge.

Cento

after reading poems by Billy Collins and Kim Addonizio

In the lamplight, and the smoke-thick air
when we have compared everything in the world,
I remember the quick, nervous bird of your love,
and how emotionally unavailable you are.
On top of all the copies of *Lolita* tossed into
a parking lot bonfire somewhere in Texas,
I want to confirm your worst fears about me.
Love me when you can't find a decent restaurant
open anywhere. I want to be a failed seed,
the kind to smell things you had never touched.
I want to make crude statements involving fluids
or Saran-Wrap you to a bedpost in New Orleans.
Praise having a body to be unhappy in.
Move like a hinge in the air above our bed
down a road that will never lead to Rome, not even Bologna.
I want it flimsy and cheap.
There will be canned chili and Fritos,
before I proceed like a polar explorer
near some blue hydrangeas instead of slouching in a café
ignorant of the word for ice.
For you I undress down to the sheaths of my nerves.
I love it when you tie me up with ropes using the knots
I learned in Boy Scouts.
I love your pain, it's so competitive.
Into every life a little ax must fall.
What a model of self-containment you could be,
but your orgasms could peel wallpaper,
so acrobatic in your welcomes.
Some men will try on your black fishnet stockings in a hotel in Berlin.
I lost you like a grape jawbreaker,

and there is nothing left to do.
Your fog-light descends from the stratosphere.
You are so beautiful and I am a fool.

Duet

Don't force this.
        I'm not praying
to every statue. I'm not going to learn
Latin.

This is what I want you to see:
        I grew up not going to church.
My grandfather was a Baptist minister.
My father didn't like
        going to church. I didn't go.

You want to marry a bad Catholic?
Those nuns are right. Don't have a bad
Catholic. I want you. Don't
force this.

I was his baby girl.
        I felt lost. No
        grounding, nothing. Look at my brother.
Getting out of his car on the freeway to
fistfight.

I'm not trying to get to heaven, but you go ahead.
        I want you to get your heaven. I'm in
action,
not wondering about the afterlife. Anyway, more attendance
doesn't mean more spiritual.

The last guy,
he gave me
        what I always lacked.

Even though he cheated, he showed me
a spirituality I never had. I pray for
myself, for you.

I don't need confirmation.
                    You want our children in
Catholic School? Fine. Don't
expect me to go to your church
every Sunday.

I want a family not like what I knew.
My childhood—fractured.
            If you're at home
watching football, and I'm taking our children
to Sunday school, what do you think they will
say?

What can make us stronger?
I would love to talk of how we can grow together.
Diversity. My faith
welcomes this. It's not Neapolitan ice cream.

You know the answer. How can you justify
yourself when questions will fly?
You make it up as you go. You want
to be a good father?

Plenty of
            married people
            have different religious faiths. I need
something else spiritually, but that doesn't
mean we can't co-habitate.

We all need ritual. I want
to go to heaven. I need you
to believe in Jesus.

There are plenty of bad Catholic men.
One, you already met. Why is it fair for me
to become another? I want a family. I know
how your family was.

Believing is not a leap
of faith. You have to believe.
It doesn't have to end this way.
Please.

Sending You a Poem

If I don't send you another poem,
I realize as I walked along the nature trail
on South Padre Island,
a blue heron standing,
a migrating oriole in the grass.

If I don't send you another poem,
you will demand more wine–
that Santa Rita Reserva from Chile
I accidently left in the trunk,
more stops for valley watermelons,
more boiling of peas to end your allergies.

And today is the first of May.
I don't have crepe streamers to tie around a pole
or money to buy you a new Corvette
even though you already have a Corvette,

and so what else is there to do
other than save a turtle
or watch sand collect along the park road
that ends ahead.

If I write you another poem,
I would fly like a black-bellied whistling duck
above the trees.
If I don't write you another poem,
I would die off the jetty four dollars poorer.

The Dr. Seuss poem I sent you last week
is looking better,

to rhyme like that in front of a high-definition
TV at the hotel is more taxing than baptizing a baby.

Actually, why don't you forget all the poems
I've ever written and splurge for surfboards
down the street?

We would never return here
with your drunken parents,
I thought to myself even though
every hour of the light and dark is a miracle
every cubic inch of space is a miracle
and the sea, the fishes, the motion of waves,

the miracle bonanza are lines I lifted
from a Walt Whitman poem
I read only a few minutes ago, by the way–

the Brooklyn poet whose birthday is soon
whose construction site of a book I
never opened in grade school,
not after my perilous journey across
the mountainous slopes of Beowulf.

Anna from The Woodlands, Texas

I wish to learn you more about me,
I was born on January 1984.
My ambitions consist
to create the strong happy family.
I would like sincerity honesty
directly concerning me. I the gentle
person. I hate lie.
I wish to learn you more
better and to open
talents to find beauty.
I have no children, was not married.
Slender is my growth and weight.
A breast, a waist, and hips accordingly.
Here, the men drink and spend for nothing
own life. I hope your day
is solar and cheerful. Forgive that I
used a city of your country. I tried to use
my city. I live in Orel, Russia.
I hope that I have not offended
you. Until tomorrow.

Oysters, Turquoise, Squash Blossomed

Not from The Woodlands—
not you.
   Did your mother make you
another Anna Karenina?
   I'm surprised the dating site
will not accept Orel, Russia.
   China is good though
I like Asian women.
   You are a fifty-year-old man
working for the mafia?
   Trust is difficult.
I think only
   more is hidden?

Forgive
but my name is not Karenina.
   I do not know any of China.
Forgive but to me it is very ridiculous
as you speak that
I work fifty years on mafia (laughter).
   I do not play with you
in games.
   I seriously adjusted women
   and me games
and flirtation are not necessary.
   I would want that you understood it!

I'm a mechanical engineer
   who did not enjoy college.
Very tough—everyone smarter.
   I paint but not now. I crosshatched

in pen and ink too,
      a tree outside my window
protected by chicken wire.
I don't have time in my real life
      to find women. No pen pals.

I'm good luck—good heart, romantic,
loyal, sincere
          woman honest
I need to belong to
     one man in the deep blue
sea. I agree that an ideal woman
      is like a chef in the kitchen, a lady in the society,
and loving in bed. I try that my glamour
     and femininity
reflect around my home in the street
     in the society.
I like to find out you better.

     I'm a baby from March.
Pisces. I read like a Pisces
     funny
imaginative.
     Sort of like James Taylor.
Do you know American music? I traveled selling pumps
for things like
     commercial laundry machines
hotel to hotel
     city to city. I met a secretary
once in Orlando, Florida.
Drinks led to endless bowls of food.
     We opened each other
     like oysters.

I remember a bed
　　　　turquoise and squash blossomed.

I like to do bowling.
　　　　I decided to draw
when my mother was lost
　　　　in road transport incident
which brought down a lorry.
　　　　I painted for twenty years
in summer or autumn.
　　　　Do you like to dance ever?
With me ever? Waltz and tango?
I cannot wait for the letter
　　　　like a child waiting
for a gift.
　　　　It is very a pity
to me
　　　　but I finish.
Wait.

Esther from Lynn Nottage's *Intimate Apparel*

Dear,

I should have run his mouth through my Singer.
He was the deacon's son,
a Mulatto who dug in Panama, cut stone
to sleeve two oceans together. He wrote
me letters, paying ten
cents for the writing, fifteen
extra for fluffier language.

I wrote him back at the ten-cent rate
humming a rag
down Orchid Street, buying
imperial silk regular
like the ice man.
I sewed gabardine singing
the spirituals, found strength
in the hallelujah, in the glory
of Scottish wool.

After we married, we bedded on my quilt
hidden with my beauty parlor dream
until I ripped at the patches of savings
one night, believing his lies. He had
relations with Mayme, my piano-playing
friend with her robe always tattered,
who stuffed the money
in his smoking jacket. There were no
more illustration books of valenciennes
lace, of gardenia ball corset.

Don't be like me at thirty-five.
I came to Manhattan tapping my foot
too long ago. The fabric from these docks,
those clients off 5th Avenue were the cloth
keeping me four yards together in magenta red.
I was a virgin then, a colored woman beaded
with too many hopes, and I have returned
to that rented flat wanting separate
lives again. I wrote this letter
fifty cents later, to you, hoping you exist,
great-granddaughter.

Geisha

These nicknamed men,
                    they aren't looking for porcelain around Japan.
They aren't looking for antique bronzes: just one-night jack stands.
They aren't thinking about their seed on a kimono, or these broken
bits of concrete from the bombed factories. Their Gucci boots
occupy the front door sleeker than my dogs.

But I was later proved wrong: Blue Bear outbid
the others for my *danna.*
                    Cher doux ours bleu—
the truffle that preserved my sunflower oil. He kept me from eating
charcoaled squid in graveled dirt. He had tufts of hair
higher than the cliffs at Normandy beach. He whisked me to his cave–
a farmhouse south of Provence. We saw movies, Judy Garland,
and I swear he growled at the wicked witch and those flying monkeys.
Who would have thought a geisha could survive in France?
I wore black scarves around the village and caught fish
from the river and carried them to market in town.

Time for me is a jigsaw puzzle, now, years later, pieces scattered
upside down in an unlucky frame, the misfortune of Blue Bear's
cancerous death is a crooked edge and now this moment,
        this dance back to Kyoto
is a piece of movement that doesn't fit.
                            I'm addicted,
old Japan, to your spiderworts, your pickled sour plums,
                your eyebrows of cooled paulownia twig,
        your drink of sake fantasy.
I will nurture my little cub–*mon petit ourson bleu*—
in your land held by silver thread
            interwoven in a brocade of folded
                rusts and golds.

Mall Encounters

I drive underneath you, park,
and ride the escalator from *LL Green*
on Friday afternoon, ready for purchase,
poised, when waterfalls from the decorated
ceiling are shut-off and echoes
swallow walls. Boutique wagons I remember
from dotted Impressionist paintings of Paris
become real and barricade the corridor.
The world of you is these games...marked-down shirts
that look like Marc Chagall canvasses, TVs with pixeled
fantasies, and mannequins undraped and curved
like fleeting memories. You have a middle-eastern
woman kidnap my hands with salt from a distant sea.
Then body butter. A smear of aloe vera
and chamomile reveals veins.
She entices me with another amulet from guess-where
before I escape, and find a Nordstrom's pianist, cracked
and caught between concerto sheets. I ride up further,
and see your restaurant touching chunks of seafood,
steamed, out of its shell, atop bits of avocado,
riding on little mountains in cylinders under tangerine
light. You call that *crab sex*. After I finish a sandwich,
the pianist vanishes. I create distance between us, finally,
towards home, discounted, and didn't think
of you, bags unopened. I breathe again and fall asleep.

Reminiscing About Matchsticks

Remember the best ones from nine thousand years ago?
We rubbed two together with our hands
causing a resistance between two bodies
we later learned was friction, and a fire
ensued inside that cave, our cores warmed,
we roasted what I killed. We survived the winters.

Where have the 1800s gone? We made small strips
of wood and paper tipped with a combustible material.
We lived in France for a while and upgraded to phosphorus.
Later, we moved to America and found twelve in a book.
We struck them using the tips of our fingers
against a narrow oxidizing landing strip that I
will never forget.

Have you forgotten what happened last summer?
The generic-jacketed ones had camped in an amber
rust candle plate cussing and swapping stories about nothing.
They punched plumeria candles across the walnut
grains of our Queen Anne table. They avoided fallen rose
petals, salt granulars, and sudden plateaus of newspapers.
They even yanked a wagon of incense from Bangalore.

Yesterday they rode from San Antonio in a box
labeled Little Rhein Steak House.
Nick's Fishmarket swam downstream from Chicago
and rendezvoused with The Daily Grind—
a local guide for the artic journey across the porcelain
tundra of our bathroom. They climbed the toilet basin
towing a candle layered in gardenia, seminole rain, and eggplant.
Certainly, it was an adventurous time to be alive.

Today, I am thinking about the extinguished ones of the past,
their brief little lives caused us to survive, and rescued us
from the jaws of boredom. I am even thinking about the future—
we could fly them to another planet, a place we can only guess,
to start over again, and tell stories around a campfire,
stories we can only imagine.

Black Scarf

We were dancing salsa and I
wasn't leading and sometimes
you slid down unannounced.

          After your ends
untwisted, I'd scoop you up
from the Tube-station tiles.

Or I'd drive back to the restaurant
after you embraced the chair
either in disgust or ecstasy
a little longer than I thought
after hearing my poem—a rant
about retail sales that tore
your 100% cashmere face
that I caressed and touched
like nothing ever before.

You U-turned back to Harrods
hoping to lose yourself in the returns
of Men's Casuals, hoping you'd kiss
a poodle with Christina Aguilera

or strangle another dancer
like your hand-painted, silk
aunt did with Isadora Duncan.

I'll forget
poems that recognize your other life
necked around Robin as you zip
along Brompton Road in a Batmobile.

Let's resurrect ourselves
from the fringe of oblivion
because I feel
oblivious and cold.

Let's unclench
the fingers of silent darkness that knitted
us apart.
We'll mirror ourselves
on the floor–a delight for any jeweled queen.

Little Drownings

Mangbetu Harp

A little drowning happens
when you hold up an instrument
like a baby
her bottom like a hull,
stitched until wood begins her torso
even if you wore a life preserver.
Listen to Africa. The tide won't
catch you in a jetty, you won't drown,
instead will carry you to some place where
a thing that makes music is art,
suspends in a dance behind glass, silent air,
casts sinew from her neck, her smooth holes
wanting to cry out, eyelids open, wild,
ready to feed ears for years, the water where
you went before is now foamy, breathless.

Muhammad Ali

In Chicago, on the South Side,
I learned to ride a bicycle,
perhaps not unlike the one he had stolen
that launched his story.
I rode the alleyways unknowingly
on a journey to his heart.

I began as a patrol boy
working a small vein
near his house
surrounded by an iron fence
imbedded in a concrete wall.
I couldn't break through before
heading south for the gift of a better education.

To Louisville, I had pedaled
over the speed bumps
of selling pumps until my reflector
caught a glimpse of him sitting at a table
signing autographs with trembling hands,
unable to connect words,
watching his daughter fight.

In Houston, the treads of my tires
well worn now,
I rounded into a curve
the ravages of his walk
to the pitcher's mound,
his fists clutching two baseballs
that he gave children who had less

than I was given when this trip
began thirty years ago.

When he shadowboxed,
when he made finger bunnies,
when the children threw
what he could no longer throw,
that is when my bike found a ventricle,
a rhythm to his life
that made me ride arms outstretched,
made me crumble over the handlebars.

The Bio

I created this literary magazine,
therefore, submitting here is a given
because I'm a word-maker-upper.

*Fragments in the Lives of Mythological
Gods* was nominated for a Pushcart Prize
and doing this has unleashed
other nominations.

Currently, I'm a first year PhD candidate
and understand the power of language
and how it's used.

My poodles have won costume prizes.
I groom them myself if I'm not
studying and practicing Buddhism,

or skiing on slopes of hotdog
wordslinging. I usually
paint in mud.

Before that, I was a film actress
and a foreign ambassador to Tahiti,

but my focus has shifted lately to
photography which reveals the mystery
of hair on the back of peoples' necks.

Ten years after high school, I fell
apart, being paranoid is no big deal.

Now I'm protected by mirrors
and friends both two- and four-legged.

I'm ready to face my brother and sister
now that the pieces are on paper.

Coffee really helps with the demons.
And the poems just speak for themselves.

Ten Ways of Looking at My Boring Life

I.   My boring life walks into a bar.
        They don't have any water, so he leaves.

II.   A rice cake is tasteless, lightweight.
        My boring life eats a bagful daily.

III.   "Eat hamburgers without pickles, order
        waffles at Waffle House," he whines.

IV.   The lake is frozen.
        My boring life tries to skate with dull blades.

V.   A man and a woman romp
        at the Motel 6.
        A man and a woman and my boring life sit
        in the Motel 6 lobby playing gin rummy.

VI.   "Turn on the T.V.," screams my boring life.
        "I miss *General Hospital*. What will happen
        to Laura and Rick?"

VII.   My boring life is no full service rest area.
        No bathrooms, no picnic tables, no vending machines
        with raspberry shortbread cookies. There are definitely
        no vending machines.

VIII. The blackbird sits on a limb and laughs
        at my boring life. He starts reading poetry.

IX.   My boring life wears a polyester blended
        shirt without a pocket. Every day in Iowa.

X.   A mermaid sat on a rock combing her hair.
When she saw my boring life on the beach,
she dove into the water.

Curry

I met you across from a circle of stainless steel
and aluminum, you didn't say anything, just stared straight
ahead, despite shiny reflections on the tiled floor. If only this
space between us was closer with potato curry from a Zebra
pot made from scrap metal, even though my heart is painted
from a small village, torn apart and roofless. Basmati rice
would stir using a Samson spoon currently spot welded to pans,
I wouldn't mention the cow dung, I would find Royal Diamond cups
for tea. I wouldn't say Blue Diamond, you'd know that curse,
that bad luck and death, I want to show you structure, boron crystalline,
like the Hope Diamond, red phosphorescence that wasn't stolen.
You're a Hindu goddess like Sita, and I'm not afraid of wild dogs
or trips to Russia, I've got two strainers, two spatulas and
plenty of tin and teaspoons. I'm ready to nourish
you—no longer a statue, your head crowned with sharply cut
leaves. If only you would open your Buddhist mouth of stucco,
traced with polychrome, we could reach nirvana.

Wrestling

for Eddie Fatu, who died at 36 of a second heart attack

"He speaks English!" the kids quipped.
We always knew him howling something
bloodthirsty, gorilla-pressing his way as Umaga,
the "Samoan Wrecking Machine" thrusting
his taped thumb in his opponent's throat.

He doesn't take ten dollars for an autograph.
"Use it for presents for your parents,"
the bulldozer says in a rock 'n' roll T-shirt,
sneakers, no war paint.

He savate kicks, swings,
and turnbuckle powerbombs us
with a two-handed chokelift.
He becomes that nerve hold,
the spectacularly unfathomable.

Someday he'll tag what is sweet
when we come looking for trouble again.
He'll lie smack down on the mat,
his tattooed stomach feuding under stars
of lights, like a childhood bully, dispatched.

Frog Meditation Protest

They're cleansing their faces with rainwater.
They're clutching their legs against their
stomachs and their hearts are beating a little
faster as a sign of the bitter coldness.

But they don't wear raincoats and galoshes
as surely as their mother would've told them
before leaping to school or winter recess.
And they aren't saying their prayers.
With the multitude of palm trees tussling,
there is no way they are saying their prayers.

You can still have the water-dribbled window
and the soggy grass and the bird bath. You
can have the sanctuary of your backyard
even if you're locked inside, a sea away
from these drenched croakers.

And speaking of nature's abundant beauty,
I'm a warm, lyrical blanket of leaves to tuck them into bed.
I'm a pond of calmness until the sky drains empty.
I'm also a net that catches horseflies.

I'm also the lather from Thich Nhat Hanh's
meditative words. However, I don't
have the sanctuary. You can have the sanctuary.
The frogs are still cleansing their faces.
By now, their mother must know they're lost.
The frogs are still in a fetal hysteria.
Their legs are still clutched against their stomachs.
Their legs are forever stuck against their stomachs.

Their hearts are beating even faster now,
and unbelievably without their raincoats
and their galoshes and somehow
above your soundless walkways.

Mexico

Quiet clouds are troubadours
dancing toward me in baroque joints.
I've lain above her now, too many years.
The spray of bougainvillea,
her voice groused deep in pockets
sad jeaned, hands roping my softest contours.

I've seen allure in her face post hippied,
touching my face before she whispered,
echoed something or nothing.
The stencil much of her eyes jazzed,
grandeur colonnaded in the gulf
between pleasure and agony.

I've played against her greenhouse,
a one-man banjo band far along in the agave.
Lifted past hot-springed pools
and punched-in lanterns, piñatas
and German cafés, our mural of lips
have met and parted, we are skeletons again.

Going to a San Miguel Poetry Retreat in January

I am not going to San Miguel
or any city in Mexico to write
poetry.

Not in January or any month
if I had a choice. Why January
to visit San Miguel?

No funny airport security
in León, no buttons to push
for a random green or red.

I will go to a British pub instead,
down the concrete sidewalk
slightly above sea level a block away

and watch a football game on Sunday.
There are no famous priests here,
or parrots eating Azteca soup.

I know other poets will write
with renewed vigor when they visit
San Miguel in January,

inspired by parades along cobbled
streets, by ringing the cathedral bell,
and karaoke of the Bee Gees.

How wonderful not to rack
my brain on how to say *bacon*
in the hotel dining room.

The huge language dam will open
to order a southwest brunch, eggs
scrambled, words flowing like waves.

And after the game, I will not have
to critique poems for hours in a room
with a heater turned up to eleven.

There is no need to linger at the Diego Rivera
mural in a stairwell or photograph
how light sculpted statues
in the courtyard. I will walk
home as if the destination is
the greatest botanical garden

the Dalai Lama ever saw. I will
see beyond my upstairs window
in a direction that will never

lead to hot springs gushing
from *la gruta*, not even
towards a ghost town.

Meth Hotel

Checking in?
Welcome to our little villas in La Palma
Breathe in our crystal air coves
Want a wake up call?
Eat Fruit Loops here in a few hours
Need a shuttle to our Disneyland?
Cook in our kitchenettes
Burn our complimentary solvents and Sudafed
Block the ether-like odors with extra towels
Avoid anxiety of the yellow haze
Come down, sip some cocktails
Booby-trap the room at no additional charge
Forget the phosphine-gassed walls
Suppress the paranoia of security cameras
                    we whip creamed the lenses
Enjoy our property at no personal risk
Blast off the roof
Smoke ice with other guests
Evacuate if necessary
Ask for bullets at the front desk
Borrow one of our guns
Fill the chamber
Mouth the barrel
Ready to check out?
Squeeze the trigger

Houdini

The perfect jam of living

is burial in your own bronze coffin.

Speaking, yes, I can talk

now without an escape.

I have spiritual secrets beyond

any mid-section blow even though

I collapsed onstage once. What do you

make of such revelations?

They levitate in mediums unlike before

when we were all human.

Would you open your cuffed

mind just this one time? The cornerstone

of my act is no longer needles

held together with thread

that I could've explained.

They're truths pooled

in the middle of your throat.

I'm still submerged as you would

feel holding your breath

under a body of water.

Despite my last spoken words,

I'm still fighting.

Fuzzy Math

for Erica Lehrer

You have already spoken
many times over
since the root
of your writing
equals light squared
with mass. A body
that accelerates and loses itself.
You are still *you*.

You want a formula?
Why count months before
you're completely disabled?
Forget the summary of days.
I will talk to your lungs
if you forget to breathe.
I will scream at your Swedish
heart if you stop.

Apologies That I've Already Made

When the angel food cake absorbed paint from the wall. When I wandered from home to Market Street after you fell asleep. When we missed the sunrise part of the mountain even though it was still afternoon. For traffic. For being here. I don't know how to make trees. For forgetting your name. That you hate roses. That you left the Renuzit in the breezeway. That I swallowed some. About wanting to speak to you about the slight damage to my lungs even though it was not quite pneumonia. That you sold the farm. When I got lost. That I couldn't find the band saw. Or the Phillips head. For snow that closed my driver's ed. For the hurricane. For bricks that fell with embedded glass. For babbling before the collision. That you blew your brains out. For my behavior at Easter service at the football stadium in Splendora. For dinner afterwards at the Golden Corral. That I couldn't get it up. That you thought I was a nice man. That you were busy, not ready. That your screwedupness is directly proportional to your prettiness. That my father drove you to prom. For sitting in the backseat. For being so unapologetic. That my brother screwed the tenant. For being happy he scored. For saying their hair is blue. Concerning rocks thrown in your backyard. For remembering. For pulling the chair away from Charles Singer in choir. For your anchovies. For refusing to buy your cigarettes. For not dumping you sooner. For singing "Scarborough Fair." Breaking your hockey stick. For dropping the Frisbee because you made me laugh. For snagging the fishing line. For catching nothing. For not thinking. That I said *fuck.* For the last sentence. For not making a sentence. For sitting in the trashcan. For face washing you. For the blood sugar. For the cartilage in my left knee. For clipping the wrong end of a cigar. For being overly gracious and my subsequent anger. For forgiving you. For losing you. For hurting you.

On the Occasion of My Boring Death

after César Vallejo

I will die in Houston on an overcast afternoon
on a day I've already forgotten.
I will die in Houston and who really cares
maybe it's a Monday.

I will wear a plain T-shirt, Levi's jeans,
and Dockers' shoes with navy socks.
A Folgers can will hold the ashes of my cremation
although Maxwell House will do
if the coffee grounds you removed are caffeinated.

At the reception, you will search for an extended metaphor
with deviled eggs
and rebirth that somehow I never really understood
since there won't be enough paprika.
There is never enough paprika.

John Denver will play "Take Me Home, Country Roads."

You will bring potato salad that won't be German potato salad.
That recipe has always been screwed up.
Your memory of me saying I liked it before isn't wrong,
I had just lied.

You will choose unscented flowers instead of my favorite,
stargazer lilies. They remind you of your father's death.

Voices will begin to subside and leave early. Mosquitoes
will bite the children playing in the backyard.
And who can blame them?

Rain will begin to fall as friends climb into their hybrid cars,
drowsy. My witnesses will remain in the wake–
the record player, the guppies in the tank, the leftovers...

Goodbyes from My House

The palmetto bugs say their goodbyes
even though they never met you.
The curl of the tuna-can lid,
the roof where they live
is shaped as goodbye.

The curvy chocolate syrup drawn
in the German-Chocolate-Cake
martini is an erotic goodbye.
The coconut flakes conspire in the goodbye.
A sort of ménage a trois invitation–and goodbye.

The dying ivy plant hanging in the kitchen
says goodbye.
The brown stain that arrived on the ceiling Thursday
should say goodbye.
The wicks of the candles say *so long* but mean goodbye.
The prostitutes painted in the Toulouse-Lautrec coasters
on the coffee table purse their lips: goodbye.
The directional flow of water flushing in both toilets
is goodbye.

Wake up! The doorbell rings at 6AM. Goodbye!

The blades of the ceiling fans turn at two speeds:
one is goodbye, and the other is a slower goodbye.
The light bulbs are long goodbye.

A prolonged goodbye is in the freezer.
Fiction is in the bedroom; the gunslinger
in Stephen King's *Dark Tower* series

constantly closes doors–
goodbye, goodbye, and more goodbyes.
Sorry you won't visit my house. Goodbye.

Forcing My Soul into Knives

A Book of Gumbo

You have to go
down to St. Louis Street
in the French Quarter and see
Big Joe about the school.
Take the Sunset Limited.
Arrive too fast and you'll never
forget where you came from.
Sit near a window so you know
what you're getting yourself into.

I.

You must chop something to pieces
to believe in the Trinity.
Sunday is as good a day as any.

II.

Stock is not water.
You have a number of things
gone and died. What is done
with the remains?

III.

Evict the tender and firm
meat cut like half moons
in the pot.
Clean trouble off the walls.

IV.

Winter time is good for
making a roux. Aunt Kary
used to say she won't slap
you for cheating, and no one
hears you cuss after the burning.

V.

Sing from the hymnal of cilantro.
Ground them as they march
forward with young,
dried sassafras.

VI.

Freeze everything.
Your guest will
arrive and after she stays
awhile, lingers,
her spoon asking
for seconds, then you know
the poem is done.

The Chili

Not the cook-off
flung at the rodeo,
but the kitchen chili where nothing
matters other than it's been
another one of those months again
that holds *r* and *y*,
forcing my soul into knives,
cutting at the start of sunset
more than I remember–garlic
and onions will feed other souls further,
beyond the leafless chinaberry tree
and into the hungry marriage of homes
overtaken by cookless friends
who stir themselves into the wide
broth of restauranteria.
Making the chili is an oath,
for so many depend on the Valrhona
cocoa, special before the ancient gods
and whoever else wants to judge–
there are too many of you.
To Katy, to Bellaire, to Spring,
the chili is unleashed before you–
within these congested freeways,
may your spoons fly.

Gumbo Season

Dark, glimmering roux, another pot
done for the Super Bowl
ten-count gulf shrimp pinked
and anchored–
a wave cutting through spreads
of chocolate greens. I'm an authentic chef
standing in my own kitchen chopping
white onions with naked hands,
slaying celery stalks, hulling poblano
peppers. Today, I sizzle pecan-smoked
sausage and come-to-Jesus cups
of stock. I'm not tenderness, rather more as leather
is standing on a wood-slatted floor, stirring.
I'm on the up-and-up over okra, a sin
not to have what is rightful. Cilantro is a song
I sing until my arm hobbles away from this spoon.
I'm orthodoxy about a Lone Star's beer dribbling
into soup. My tongue can't hitch with sherry.
My head is thick and bursts open, a robin,
yearning for flavor, cradling astonishment
and quiet apertures of those seasons before.
It's that season again when friends return,
oiled for seconds.

Pizza Dough Ode

It was hard to believe with whole wheat flour
to imagine yeast and water would fold
down into the bowl and after kneading,
there remains patience,
and if that was ever going to rise
dusted as night elbowed away the afternoon,
these two hands would descend further to beat
until smooth air charged inside and released.

Pressing and pulling apart that which
was together and now stressed,
these two hands would
certainly haven't preferred to handle
during the departure of fall by the window
overlooking the porch where the snow would
eventually need shoveling from the stairs,
and that was something else that mattered
as firmly as the back which owned the shoulders
that rose and sank.

These two hands wouldn't even know
or even guess what happens next by brushing
olive oil across your body. But others, perhaps
cannot forget you clothed forever in the bread pan,
your face struck with other ingredients or your edge.

Julia

R.I.P. February 2010

I am the hen who rented a room
at the Raven Grill, but now I've returned
to tell you what had been the most sacred:
the bread crumbs you left on the patio tables.

When you ordered the pecan-crusted chicken,
I only wanted to bury my head in the begonias. Even
the Raven Dinner was three chicken, cheese and sour
cream flautas. What the heck ever happened to the ravens?

If I had been the police, I would have ticketed
your speeding along Bissonnet. Giving you
the eye after seeing your parallel parking
was never enough to prevent an accident.

When your children said I was rooster,
I always wanted to peck at your face. I
never wanted to lay an egg to prove
them wrong.

Now I have wobbled across this bigger
road freed of your pea-sized gravel
driveway, no longer waiting for your impatiens,
and those pathetic little planters.

Up here the hours as you can imagine are better.
The smorgasbord of drugs and alcohol is endless,
sickness and the consequences,
who ever said there were any?

Men who have never cheated
on their wives drive the best cars.

We're still in jokes, the chicks write
fiction, and often, we ride by on skateboards.

A River of Blossoms

I always wanted to wear a scarf
like Isadora Duncan did
in a limousine with the bubbletop on
                        to turn around and feel marvelous
and tasteful.
I never liked my neck unprotected
                        especially in November, normally.
Chills remind me of miscarriages
                        that never happen.
I didn't believe in population control.
Jack said those Republican women
                        at the lunch wore
mink coats and diamond bracelets.
I thought a beige and white dress
                        would fill the order.
You know what I chose–
                        a pink suit with a navy collar
and a matching pillbox hat.
I loved Coco Chanel.

            * * *

It was the summer of 1969, and I was a boy that heard a sound
                        from the porch.
Waldorf Drive in Akron, Ohio,
                        fireflies caught in glass jars
with holes poked in the top for air
                        leaves caught fire
for making smoke,
            never playing past the ditch.
I brought lettuce to school for a rabbit,
            only I lost the lettuce. I showed

other children how to tie their shoes.
                     Acidy juice oozed
from garden tomatoes.
               I lined a river with stones
in a sandbox my father made.
We drove to a store and loaded the VW Hatchback
with bags of sand,
          pulling my arms,
a cracking sound, grains of powder going off from a toy cap gun,
the die-cast metal type I imagined
        after the stones in the river
weren't embedded enough to hold water.

      * * *

I saw bright yellow roses
             until Dallas
when they turned red.
              I thought, how funny.
It was a very hot day–I lost the roses
and the pale lavender asters.
   There was no water,
I thought how I wanted caviar
and France.
        I was getting pushed away
people were pulling
       my hand.
    I thought if I became blind,
if we become blind,
   then do we know about danger?

      * * *

I'm like a machine,
     I have the right parts
to serve a purpose. I dragged a hose from the house,
          then under a black cherry tree-
where the first bee stung.
        That cracking sound came
after my brother said, "I'm going to kill you."
Was that sound echoing from a Colt Detective Special
        from those cop dramas?
I didn't know how a fly could survive
       glowing in a glass jar,
or whether they named boys
who played with fire.

    * * *

All my life I never dreamed a hospital visit
        was like a river of blossoms in this suit.
What should be the best,
      I just feel is more or less
like Camelot, Jack played that music
    before going to bed, now he is a legend
when he would have preferred
        to be a man. I'm in the story too
caked up, nothing left.
      Just ask a rider-less horse.

    * * *

My father was in the Army Reserves.
      "Did you ever shoot anyone?" I asked him.
"No, I never did. But let me tell you
      a little about what bullets do."
That was the morning he was silent

after hearing my brother.
My father remembered something
                    unspoken that hung in the air
        which fell
not unlike the plastic gun that he cracked over his knee,
                    several times, unmistakably,
broken.

The Woman in Edward Hopper's *Nighthawks*

She likes the dark in the diner.

She likes this dress best–creamed-cut
maroon that exposes her arms.

She likes the light, but not the unflattering
brightness when pouty lipstick wears off
and makeup cakes.

She likes this window, a prison that wedges
seamlessly and separates two continents:

one a story that contains a man leaving his wife,
his children. Her not begging or crying

and one a street filled with skyscrapers
where every turn yields results
where storefronts display need.
She likes film noir of menace.

She likes the smell of stillness, which is crazy
and faint. Like her hair with ashes or henna.

She likes a gas station opened.
The making of what must be time on the move
and his hands no longer moving over her.

She likes January. Sidewalks aren't stressed
with clarity. So slushy, worse than skim milk.

She likes the theater with dreams so wide.
With men, circling in their hushness, sipping
their coffee or committed to murder.

Outlaw

I saw Bonnie, the waitress struggling
a long time ago in Dallas. She smoked
a cigar with eyebrows that rose up earth.

And if Clyde is buried ten miles away,
then how far does the car in the sky
ride romance?

What you love is riddled. You've
been kidnapped to write on
a little placard for his dashboard
that you're on the same wavelength.

The passenger door opens at the assaulted
gas station where the tanks are filled
and you are shotgunned out,
violent and embraced.

Madison Park

is not in New York, it's a private
park on the south side of Chicago
where I played baseball

and broke windows on condos
and city buses stopped on the other side
of a fence bordering a dirt lot

smaller than Navy Pier but smelled
like Nantucket Bay. The park breathed
with trees, had tentacles that were alleyways

I bicycled which connected to basements
where I played Ping-Pong and saw a friend
kidnaped on the way home from school.

Angela Davis was not a political activist.
She was a Manx cat never ready to muzzle
my behavior and liberated the go-go mango

sofa, and refereed marble hockey.
A girl had a hold over me with perfect-
penny skin who lived at the other end

of the park, but right down the line,
like the Gerry Rafferty song I recorded
on the tape deck, she disappeared like vapor,

and more trees were planted surrounded
by little wiry fences where the line
of throwing a ball or running the bases

was cut like shredding strips of paper
through a strip-cut shredder even though
I didn't know anyone who owned a shredder.

When I Die

Dear God:

No avoiding a party at your beach rental property.
You'll wear a ruffled silk shirt,
and claim you're not an art collector.
I was a loose speck in your kaleidoscope
telling everyone not to read romance novels
because they made people dysfunctional.
You continue to preach from those romance pages.
You're relieved and frankly, after praying many times,
my knees are relieved too, from the yuppie wood
I nailed down to replace the Berber my cat chewed up.
You'll have my friends pour water over sugar cubes
with Vermouth or whatever green liquid
you were spouting about in my last days.
No avoiding you rubbing that in though I will point out
you convinced others to plaster themselves that way.

It's not like this is the first beach house party you've thrown
because remember I know I was on the invite list
when you took the lives of my friends.
You made us read the Bible on the coffee table
before roasting the pig.
We broke the coffee table that year,
and I meant to ask if you got your deposit back.
But then I thought why would you write a check
to the landlord if you're not the landlord?
Anyway, the meat tasted bad.
Reminded me of the Rawlings
baseball glove you stole from my closet.
No avoiding the fact that you'll turn on a neon sign

which will hum in the fog, glowing *Vacancy*
in the dark after the party is over.
The sugar cubes gone, the bottles recycled.
Then comes Sunday–another day to wear jeans.

Ojo Caliente

on the way back from Taos, NM

I found your mineral spring eye
by the dotted
highway when I whispered into the iron
pool west of the Rio Grande.

These volcanic pressures eat
what I've tasted
shoved against a giant blue ceiling.

Is the natural pebble floor
this beast of vapor seeping into skin,
into blood
ebbing away what is alive?

And your soda surrounded by walls
did nothing but steam bones enough
to climb a mesa
digest what is night,
a vast unknowingness.

Should I have swallowed holy soil
cooked up in Chimayo? I would choke
and die. But I'm dying now.
And I've forgotten lithium.
Does the lithia spring pump
sulphur free,
guzzle as if there were no more rain?

The arsenic and sodium is heated,
soaks thoughts of driving off

a cliff or sleeping outside and awakening
with snakes that coil, poison or charm
exotic dreams.

If We Lived at Sarah Oppenheimer's *D-17*

you'd paint the switch plates
under the hammered aluminum roof
even though there is no electricity.

Jutting through glass and brick is what broke apart
as if snow fell and drifted against alleyways.

You'd say we're living under a white, sleek jet wing,
and I wouldn't disagree.

I don't know where you'd hang your dresses.
We've never opened closet doors together.

Windows, who ever needed windows?
You'd want rain droplets falling onto your face
even though I'd spiral into a weathered personality
disorder.

I'd want to ski a slope into the entrance
of your heart, but what I learned in
Lake Geneva, Wisconsin failed.

Every elevator pretends I'm an elephant slowly
descending into corners with busted flaps.
Yet this is where we're magnificently crashed.

You'd awaken under a rhombus lifting off mornings.
I'd crust open imbedded parallelograms,
and we'd break boundary layers under the long
neck of this swan.

Folk Song

The first note is almost struck.
A string could be picked at any moment.
You aren't hungry yet.
Think of a guest entering the shadows
in the front room of your house.
This is the minute before midnight
when she turns seventeen.
The dynamite is fused in the coal mine.
The dragon is still asleep in the cave.
The lead singer introduces the piece
with words that tell us about the rise.
We could even have an Oh, yeah. Oh, yeah.
This is the inkling a war veteran
has to hammer a ring for his wife.
This is the train conductor saying All Aboard!
This is the prelude to your first kiss with her,
your first night with someone else.
This is the section where the tracks turn green,
where lawn chairs outstretch,
when the lawyers draft your will.

The next part is the layer beneath the upper crust.
The coffee is stirred, the yokes burst on a plate.
Here the singer detours into a Paul Simon riff
or tells us how George Harrison autographed his guitar.
You begin to love a waitress with amnesia.
Photographs develop of you littering in the city dump.
Chris McCandless leaves for the wild.
This is the car driving towards the tornado.
This is the verse that puffs fire or explodes
and suddenly goes quiet.

The developers have renamed the place
after what they've torn apart.
The bridge spans thin air, but the oxygen bottles
are 3000 feet below.
This is sitting in the street for justice.
You've entered the witness-protection program in Anchorage.
So much of this song is quicksand, so much confusion-
snow in Austin, the break of a string, an appendix swells,
your friend does crack from a Coke can, the first gardenia
blooms, you leave Savannah on Christmas Day-
This is the last trimester.

The Jayco rental is almost over.
The pony is too small to ride.
This is the time to harvest corn,
dry ears in the bin.
The singer belts higher than what she sang before,
she goes down an octave or two, pleads the audience to sing.
Soap bubbles blow from the side stage.
Black sheep flock the front yard
careful not to nibble at the bodies of background vocalists.
Here is the last bit of change for the New Jersey Turnpike,
and your house echoes with haunting laughter.
The final strumming is the grave sounds we imagined.
This is what Arlo Guthrie lived for,
what rhythm we should feel like in the floorboards
before our heads are cut off.
This is the bell chime that begins a funeral
under the blood of stage lights.
This is a raccoon leaving a hollowed tree
outside a blanket of stars,
and above, or maybe inside the ribcages,
we hear the chords of each other's angels.

Notes

"Making Love to Natalie Merchant." is based on the former lead singer of a popular band called the *10,000 Maniacs*. Some of her best-known songs are "Carnival," "Kind and Generous," and "Jealousy."

"Esther from Lynn Nottage's *Intimate Apparel*." This play is about an African-American woman (Esther) who migrates from the Carolinas to New York and designs intimate apparel for the New York Society Ladies and prostitutes in the early 1900s. Since she can't read or write, she asks one of her clients to write letters to Esther's future husband. The play is modeled supposedly after the playwright's great-grandmother and actual letters.

"Black Scarf." Line 7: Tube-station is a train station of London's Underground. Brompton Road is a road bordering Harrods. Line 20: The chairman of Harrods (Mohamed Al Fayed) frequently schedules celebrities to open sales events. He invited Christina Aguilera and her poodle one year. Chris O'Donnell, who played Robin in *Batman*, arrived once in the Batmobile used in the movie. Line 23: Isadora Duncan was an influential pioneer of modern dance in the early 1900s known to wear flowing scarves. She met her tragic death on September 14, 1927 when one of her scarves entangled in the open-spoked wheel and rear axle of a moving car in Nice, France. She died a Russian citizen. Her last known words were "I am off to love."

"Mangbetu Harp" is based on seeing an anthropomorphic harp, early 20th Century, made from wood, hide, sinew, and string at The Museum of Fine Arts, Houston, Texas.

"Curry" is based on Subodh Gupta's *Untitled*, 2008, a sculpture made of welded stainless steel kitchen utensils, pots, and pans at The Museum of Fine Arts, Houston, Texas.

www.ingramcontent.com/pod-product-compliance
Lightning Source LLC
Chambersburg PA
CBHW022013090426
42741CB00007B/1018